CHILDREN'S

-Party-

CAKES

Devised and illustrated by

Clare Beaton

Kingfisher Books

CONTENTS

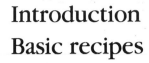

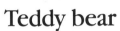

Produced by Times Four Publishing Ltd
Art and editorial direction: Tony Potter
Copy editor: Nicola Wright
Home Economist: Nicola Bereen

Kingfisher Books, Grisewood & Dempsey Ltd,
Elsley House, 24-30 Great Titchfield St, London W1P 7AD.

First published in 1991 by Kingfisher Books.
Copyright © Times Four Publishing Ltd. 1991

Colour separations by RCS Graphics, Leeds.
Typeset by C-Type, Horley, Surrey.
Printed in Spain.

BRITISH LIBRARY CATALOGUING IN PUBLICATION DATA

Beaton, Clare
    Children's party cakes.
    1. Cakes. Decoration
    I. Title   II. Series
    641.8653

ISBN 0-86272-701-4

INTRODUCTION

If you are ever stuck for new ideas for children's party cakes - or are not sure how to make novelty cakes - then this book is for you. Everything here is straightforward to make, and detailed pictures clearly explain each stage. Your children will love helping with the cooking and decorating, as well as eating the results!

Recipes

Using the easy basic sponge cake recipe on page 4, the book shows you step-by-step how to create fun and attractive cakes - for birthdays or other special celebrations.

Variations

The instructions show you how to create several variations of each basic idea. Following the same methods, you might like to try experimenting with some of your own ideas.

Decorations

There are plenty of tips on decorating your cakes too, using fondant or butter icing with simple added extras, such as wafers and sweets. Always avoid using whole nuts and sweets that could get stuck in small children's throats.

Themes

Many of the cakes can be linked to a party theme, for example a space party or circus party.

Ingredients

Ingredients are given in both metric and imperial measures. It is best to use either metric or imperial, but not a mixture of both.

Food colouring

Natural food colourings are available. When you go shopping, look at the alternatives on offer and carefully check the ingredients. Annatto, riboflavin, cochineal and beetroot red are all natural food colourings.

More ideas

At the end of this book there are several additional ideas for you to try. It might be a good idea to keep a 'Party' file of magazine cuttings for future use.

BASIC RECIPES

You will need . . .

2 x 20cm or 8"
round cake tins
150g or 6oz
  softened
  butter or
  margarine
150g or 6oz caster
  sugar
3 eggs size 3
150g or 6oz self-
  raising flour

Variations

Chocolate - add a
little hot water to
25g or 1oz of cocoa
powder and mix to a paste (or melt the same
amount of chocolate). Beat into the creamed
butter and sugar mixture.

Orange or lemon - finely grate the rind of one
orange or lemon and add to the cake mixture.
For extra flavour add a little of the juice.

Marble - divide the creamed mixture in half. Add a
little hot water to 25g or 1oz of cocoa powder and
mix to a paste. Mix into the creamed mixture. For
different colours, add a few drops of food
colouring and mix well. Place alternate spoonfuls
of the two mixtures in tins.

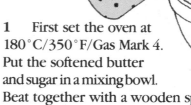

1   First set the oven at
180°C/350°F/Gas Mark 4.
Put the softened butter
and sugar in a mixing bowl.
Beat together with a wooden spoon until the
mixture is pale and creamy. Add the beaten eggs
to the mixture a little at a time, stirring well until
it is smooth.

2   Sieve the flour into the mixture and fold in
carefully until well mixed. The cake mixture
should be soft and light. Grease tins with butter or
margarine, add a little flour, shake, then empty out
(or use a pastry brush and a teaspoon of oil). You
could line deep tins with butter papers or
greaseproof paper. Pour half the cake mixture into
each greased tin and smooth until level.

3   The cake is done when well-risen and brown.
It should feel springy in the middle and be starting
to shrink away from the edge of the tin.
As an extra test, insert a warm
metal skewer into the middle
of the cake - if it comes out
clean then the cake is ready.
Turn onto wire racks to cool.

Butter icing

Butter icing can be used to stick cakes together, and to make a rough surface decoration. Use half the amount of butter to the amount of icing sugar (you can use margarine instead) e.g. 75g or 3oz of butter to 150g or 6oz of icing sugar. Beat the icing sugar into the bowl a little at a time, mixing in with the butter. If too thick to spread stir in a little milk. Use a piping bag to apply the icing, or a warm knife to spread it. As a less sweet alternative, make an icing from soft cream cheese mixed with lemon or orange juice and honey.

Fondant icing

Fondant icing is ideal for covering and modelling. Buy packets of 250g or 450g and roll out to desired thickness. Cover rolling pin with icing sugar first to prevent it sticking to the icing. When covering cakes, apply a little jam to the cake surface first to help it stick. Use your finger to mould fondant icing and cover joins, with a little water if necessary. To cover a pudding basin-shaped cake, roll out the icing into a round and then mould it round the cake. Keep fondant icing covered when not using it to stop it drying out.

Glacé icing

Glacé icing is very simple to make and covers cakes easily. Sift 150g or 6oz of icing sugar into a bowl. Add hot water a little at a time, mixing it with the sugar to make a smooth paste that is easy to spread.

Decoration

Cake decorations such as silver balls and plastic flowers, sweets, and dried or fresh fruit can all be used. Avoid whole nuts as these can choke small children. Marzipan or fondant icing can be shaped into figures.

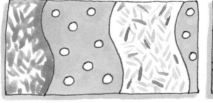

Press different shaped objects into icing while it is still soft to form interesting patterns.

You can colour icing or marzipan by adding a few drops of food colouring and kneading well, or by painting with a brush after modelling.

Press fondant icing through a garlic press to make 'hair' and 'branches'.

BASIC CAKES

You can create all kinds of novelty cakes by cutting and building with the basic shapes shown below. Stick the pieces together with jam or butter icing.

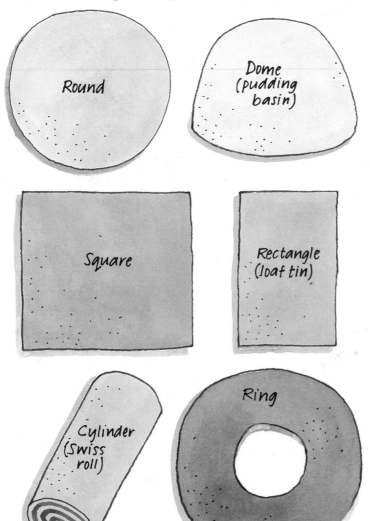

Small cakes, biscuits, ice cream cones and wafers are ideal for details such as ears and arms.

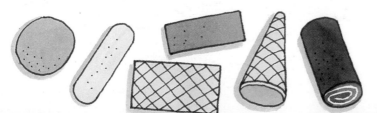

Here are two simple ideas from pieces joined together:

MONSTER CAKE

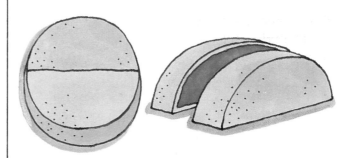

Cut a ring cake in two, slide along and stick together.

RAINBOW CAKE

Cut a round cake in two, stand up and stick together. You could cover the cake in fondant icing and paint stripes with a brush and food colouring. Or apply butter icing using a knife or piping bag.

NUMBER CAKES

Hire, buy or borrow the cake tins and use the same number of decorations on top.

Swimming pool

Use biscuit cutters to make fondant icing shapes for decoration. Sprinkle with cake decorations.

Keep models simple and bright.

Use ornaments as candle holders.

Shark fins would be fun!

If you have a party with a theme, it can be fun making a cake to match. Cover a simple shape in icing and model figures.

Chocolate logs topped with green icing make good trees.

Football

Start making your models early, a few at a time, and keep them in a tin.

Write a message with a brush and food colouring.

Ice skating

7

CLOWN

You will need . . .

1 x ½pt or 10fl oz
   pudding basin
   sponge cake
1 x 1pt or 20fl oz
   pudding basin
   sponge cake
2 x 250g or 1 x 450g
   packets of fondant
   icing
2 sponge fingers
1 ice cream cone
Food colouring
Sweets

1   Colour and roll out 300g or 11oz of icing to cover the body and for sleeves. Roll out 100g or 4oz of white icing and cover the head and sponge fingers. Press the head and arms into the body.

2   Decorate the clown's body by pressing sweets into the icing. Use sweets to make a nose and eyes. For the mouth use a short strip of liquorice.

3   Colour the remaining fondant icing orange to make hair and cut into a fringe shape. Press carefully around the head. Cut the ice cream cone to fit the head and use as a hat.

Tom is 5 today!

WITCH/WIZARD

Use biscuit cutters to make fondant icing shapes for decorations.

Happy Birthday

Make a banner from a strip of paper and two small sticks.

Cover the clown's hat in fondant icing and decorate.

You could use a bought hat.

CASTLE

You will need . . .

3 x 180cm or 7" square
    sponge cakes
4 Swiss rolls
4 x 250g or 2 x 450g
    packets of fondant
    icing
Food colouring
Liquorice
Jam

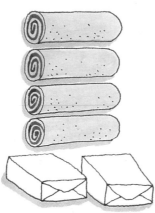

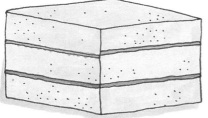

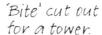

'Bite' cut out
for a tower.

You could
make the
icing a sandy colour
instead of grey.

1 Assemble the cakes in layers with jam. Cut 'bites' out of each corner. Add colouring to the icing, kneading well to mix. Roll out half of the icing and cover the cake.

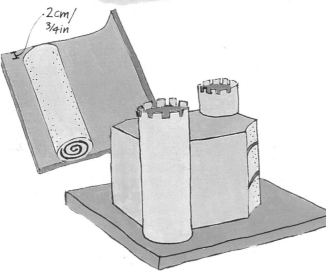

2cm/
3/4in

2 To make towers, roll out fondant icing to cover the Swiss rolls, leaving 2cm (¾in) spare at the top. Cut out squares from this, then cover each roll and stick them to the castle with jam.

3 Cut liquorice strips to make windows and a drawbridge and stick them to the sides of the castle with jam.

For the finishing touch, make flags out of paper stuck onto cocktail sticks.

FAIRYTALE CASTLE

Make this castle in the same way, placing icing-covered ice cream cones on top of the towers. Decorate the castle with bright cake decorations.

You could also add tiny toy knights.

RABBIT

You will need . . .

1 x ½pt or 10fl oz
  pudding basin
  sponge cake
1 x 1pt or 20fl oz
  pudding basin
  sponge cake
2 sponge fingers
200g or 8oz butter icing
Whipping cream
Brown or black
  food colouring
Liquorice sweets

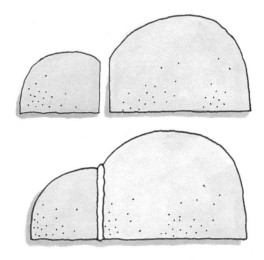

1   Cut a slice off one side of each cake and stick the cakes together using a little of the butter icing.

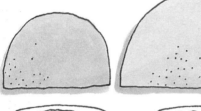

2   Divide the icing up and colour one batch. Use both batches to cover the body, using a knife or piping bag. Cover the sponge fingers and press in place on the cake.

3   Make the rabbit's face from sweets. But before serving, arrange a big blob of fluffy cream for a tail.

For a birthday you could place candles in holders and stick them along the back of the cake. You could model a carrot out of marzipan or fondant icing and place it next to the rabbit for a good finishing touch.

CAT

Wafer
ears↓

Match your pet's markings if you have one.

Sponge
finger
tail
↓

MOUSE

Biscuit
ears↓

Liquorice or
string tail↓

TEDDY BEAR

You will need . . .

2 round sponge cakes
4 mini Swiss rolls
230g or 8oz butter icing
Small amount of
   fondant icing
Yellow and red
   food colouring
Sweets

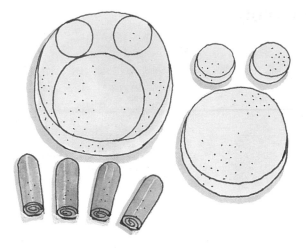

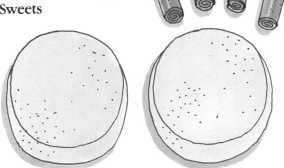

1 Cut one cake into a smaller round for Teddy's head and two little rounds for his ears.

2 Assemble Teddy's body on a tray or board. Stick all the parts together with butter icing. Colour the rest of the icing, and cover the whole body, using a knife or piping bag.

3 Stick on sweets or fondant icing to make eyes, nose and mouth. Colour the fondant icing, cut a bow tie out of it, and decorate with silver balls.

LADYBIRD

SUN

Use liquorice to make antennae and spots.

Surround a cake with sponge fingers and ice cream wafers.

PANDA

Make like the Teddy, but cover in black and white fondant icing.

Add candle 'buttons' down Teddy's tummy.

ROCKET

You will need . . .

1 Swiss roll
1 ice cream cone
6 ice cream wafers
2 x 250g or
    1 x 450g
    packets of fondant
    icing
Liquorice sweets
Blue food colouring
Small amount of glacé
    icing (optional)
Candles and holders
    (optional)

1   Divide the icing in half and add drops of colouring to one half, kneading well to mix. Roll out to about 3mm thick. Roll out the rest of the icing.

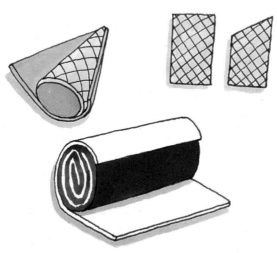

Decorate with sweets and liquorice

2   Carefully wrap the blue icing around the ice cream cone. Cut one corner off each wafer. Cover the Swiss roll with white icing, pinching the edges to seal.

3   Assemble the rocket by standing the Swiss roll on end on a plate or board. Push the wafers in evenly around the base. Place the cone on top and pinch icing together.

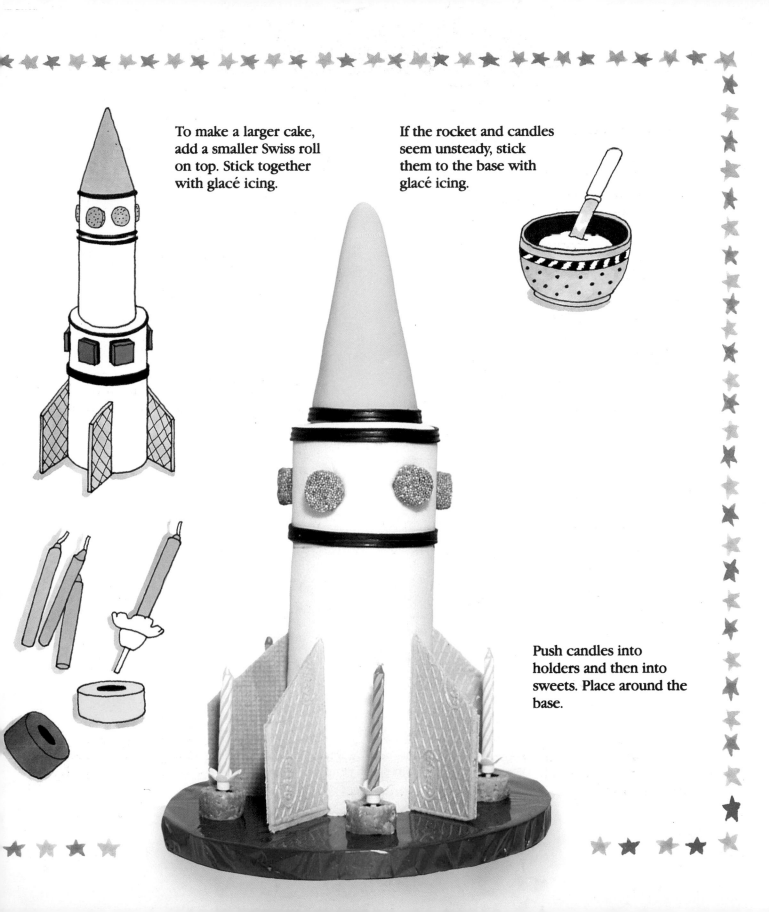

To make a larger cake, add a smaller Swiss roll on top. Stick together with glacé icing.

If the rocket and candles seem unsteady, stick them to the base with glacé icing.

Push candles into holders and then into sweets. Place around the base.

You will need . . .

1 x 20cm or 8" round
    marble sponge cake
2 x 250g or
    1 x 450g
    packets of fondant
    icing
2 sponge fingers
3 food colours
Sweets, liquorice and
    cake decorations

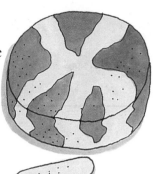

1   Cut the cake into two halves and put them back to back. Cut each sponge finger to fit as the body of the butterfly.

2   Divide the icing into three equal parts and colour each piece by kneading well with a few drops of food colouring. Roll out and cover the top of the cake and the sponge fingers.

3   Decorate the butterfly with sweets and pretty cake decorations. Make the antennae from pieces of liquorice.

BAT CAKE

You can add liquorice 'wing lines' if you like.

Follow the same instructions as for the butterfly, using a marble sponge cake and sponge finger. Cut three 'bites' out of the straight edge of each half of the cake. Place together, position body, and cover with black icing. Add icing ears and sweet eyes.

DINOSAUR

You will need . . .

2 round sponge cakes
2 sponge fingers
200g or 8oz butter icing
3 ice cream wafers
Sweets
Food colouring

Sandwich two cakes together with butter icing.

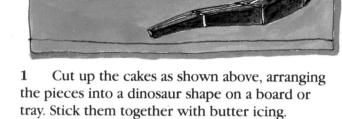

Cut the cake as shown. Use piece number 1 for the head, following through to number 7 for the tail.

1 Cut up the cakes as shown above, arranging the pieces into a dinosaur shape on a board or tray. Stick them together with butter icing.

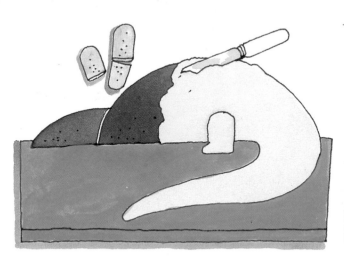

2 Liberally cover the whole dinosaur with butter icing. Cut the sponge fingers in half and press into position as feet. Also cover these with icing.

3 Cut the wafers into three triangular pieces and stick them along the top of the dinosaur. Decorate with sweets, using two large ones for the eyes.

Make tiny trees out of green fondant icing and chocolate logs.

WHALE

Silver foil

SHARK

Wafer teeth, fin and tail

Sharks, whales and snowmen are all easy to model.

SNOWMAN

Raisins and fondant icing details.

Coconut snow

BUS

You will need . . .

2 x 2lb or 1kg loaf
    tin sponge cakes
2 Swiss rolls
    2 x 250g or
    1 x 450g
    packets of fondant
    icing
Red and black food
    colouring
Sweets
Jam

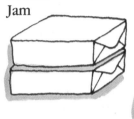

1   Make the bus body by cutting a quarter off one cake and sticking both cakes together with jam. Cut sections out of the Swiss rolls as shown and stick in position as wheels.

2   Colour 300g or 11oz of the icing red and roll out to cover the bus. Then colour 100g or 4oz of icing black, roll out and cover the wheels. From the remaining white icing, measure and cut a strip for the windows.

3   Stick sweets on for hubcaps and headlights. With any remaining icing cut out passengers, paint them with food colouring and press onto the windows.

LORRY

By changing the shape of the top edge you can make different vehicles. For example, using a smaller piece of cake on top you can make a lorry. Put small bags of sweets or raisins on the back.

PRAM

Making a pram is just as easy. Decorate it with silver balls and strips of fondant icing pressed into frills.

Liquorice handle

Make faces from sweets and strips of fondant icing.

MORE IDEAS

Here are three more cakes easily made and decorated.

CATERPILLAR CAKE

You will need about
4 Swiss rolls for this cake.

Swiss rolls, cut
into pieces and
halved.

Cover a small sponge
pudding basin cake
in fondant icing
for the head.

CHEESE AND MICE CAKE

Buy or make
sugar mice.

Use two quarters of a round sponge cake stuck
together with jam or butter icing.
Gently press 'holes' into yellow fondant icing
with the end of a wooden spoon.

TRAIN CAKE

Use mini Swiss rolls to make this cake.

Engine

Cut one Swiss
roll in half to
fit on top of
another.

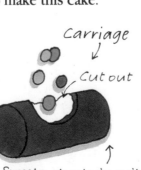

Carriage

Cut out

Sweets stuck in with
butter icing.

Liquorice or chocolate
finger track

Make a carriage
for each child.